TAKING

YOUR

RELATIONSHIPS

OFF

CRUISE CONTROL

MINDSET FOR IMPROVING FIVE
KEY RELATIONSHIPS IN YOUR LIFE

JASON & TINA MARIE SCOTT

Certified Life & Relationship Experts

Founders of Legendary Relationship

Printed in the United States of America

Taking Your Relationships Off Cruise Control

For permission requests, contact:

Principles Work
4801 Southwick Dr. Suite 101 #1020
Matteson, IL 60443
legendaryrelationship.com

First Printing, 2025
ISBN 979-8-9910034-4-5 (Paperback)
ISBN 979-8-9910034-5-2 (eBook)

Library of Congress Catalog Number: 2025917723

Ordering Information
Special discounts are available for bulk purchases by corporations, associations, and other groups. For more details, visit legendaryrelationship.com or email us at team@legendaryrelationship.com

CONTENTS

INTRODUCTION

MAYBE, JUST MAYBE, IT'S NOT THEM AFTER ALL

What if you've been looking in the wrong direction this whole time? What if the reason your relationships keep hitting the same wall isn't because of them... but because you keep thinking the same way, speaking the same way, and acting the same way, expecting them to change? Some might even call that the insanity factor. Let's get off this merry-go-round and go find the missing pieces to successful relationships.

When you finally understand why things happen the way they do and where you fit into that puzzle, that's the moment when the puzzle pieces start fitting together. That moment changes everything. And it starts here.

Welcome to changing every relationship in your life, from the one you have with yourself to the ones with your family, friends, colleagues, and intimate partner. If you've found yourself, a time or two, feeling frustrated, disconnected, or unsure about how to communicate better and improve your relationships, you're not alone. We've all been there. However, we're here to tell you that everything you need to shift the dynamics of your relationships already lies within you, not outside of you. Yes, it really begins and ends with you.

You might say you're fine, and it's the other folks that keep up the drama. Well, we hate to break it to you, but that mindset is the reason for the drama and inharmonious relationships.

Your mindset is the lens through which you view every interaction, every person, and every situation. Change how you see things, and the way people respond to you will change, too. It may sound simple, but it requires intention, work, and persistence. The key to creating better relationships in every area of your life lies in your ability to shift your perspective and make small but impactful changes in how you engage with others. Although we've created the parameters of our relationships, we can indeed recreate them without the necessity of others changing first. If we change the way we think, speak, act, and react to others, in turn, they must do the same. We often look for others or the situation to change first before we change. But unfortunately, it is just the opposite.

The purpose of this book is to help you understand that the only person you have the power to truly change is yourself. This is accomplished through shifting your mindset. As you shift your mindset, you'll start to notice how your relationships evolve around you. Whether it's understanding your value, setting healthier boundaries, learning to communicate more effectively, or respecting different points of view, we hope that this book helps you improve your relationships in ways that feel aligned with who you truly are.

Why Does Mindset Matter?

Every relationship in your life is shaped by how you show up in it. The beliefs you hold about yourself, others, and the world around you influence the way you interact with everyone. This includes your spouse to your boss, to the cashier at the local grocery store. When you see yourself as worthy of love and respect, your relationships will naturally reflect that belief. When you believe you can create positive change, you'll see how that optimism can open doors and create opportunities for growth and connection. You get to dictate how each relationship in your life will be. Whether it's up close and personal, or at a far distance. But you get to choose which relationships are worth the work and understanding, and those that are not worth giving them a second thought for your peace of mind. But you won't have to fake it or force it. When your mindset is shifted, your life is shifted. It's like seeing things from the window of a plane, instead of viewing them at ground level.

Your mindset creates your thoughts. And your thoughts produce the things in your lives. So, if we want to change the "not so positive" relationships, we have to think and see them differently. This allows you to take control over every situation and keep your emotional well-being intact.

It's about finding the courage to look within, adjust how we approach others, and ultimately permit ourselves to see things differently so that things can be different.

In the pages ahead, we will discuss how to improve five key relationships in your life.

1. The Relationship You Have with Yourself - Because it all starts here. The awareness to show up as your best self in every relationship.

2. The Relationship with Family and Friends - Why it's essential to communicate more effectively, set & honor healthier boundaries, and improve these important connections.

3. The Relationship with Colleagues and Co-workers - Whether you're a leader or part of a team, improving your professional relationships will help you thrive at work, in your career, and life.

4. The Relationship with Money, Education, and Material Things - Your relationship with money shapes your peace of mind.

5. Intimate Relationships - Building relationships on trust, respect, and understanding. The importance of being aware and intentional when writing your relationship story.

We're excited to have you here. Together, we're going to shift the way you think, the way you communicate, and ultimately the way you connect with others. Remember, change is always possible, and it starts with you. If you're ready to put this book to work in your relationships, let's get right to it!

ONE

YOUR FIRST RELATIONSHIP AND THE ONE YOU CAN'T ESCAPE

Every relationship you've ever had, be it romantic, professional, or casual, is a reflection of this one. If it's strong, everything else has a chance. If it's shaky, nothing else will feel stable for long. And here's the plot twist: you're the only one in it.

Let's start with the basics and get straight to the truth - you are the starting point of every relationship in your life.

How you relate to yourself sets the standard for every other relationship you have - at home, at work, and in love.

When you step into the version of you that feels whole, confident, and worthy, the world starts meeting you at that level.

If the relationship you have with yourself is off - if your thoughts are critical, your inner voice is harsh, or your self-worth is rickety, then everything else you attract or engage with will reflect that. That's not judgment. That's just how energy and awareness work.

But the tricky thing about the relationship we have with ourselves is that it can disguise itself as self-love and worth. We can convince ourselves that we have self-love and worth, but the reflective relationships we encounter throughout our lives show us differently.

Unfortunately, we've been trained and conditioned to look out there (outside of ourselves) for love, validation, security, and happiness. But chasing those things outside of you will only leave you drained and disappointed. Why? Because nothing outside of you can give you what you already have inside of you.

You already have everything you need to have healthy, harmonious relationships.

Stop Waiting for the Outside to Change

We've seen it time and again, someone believes they'll finally be happy once:

- Their partner stops arguing.
- Their parents/siblings apologize.
- They get a promotion.
- Someone finally chooses them.
- They lose the weight, earn the degree, or get the ring.

But here's the hard truth wrapped in love: waiting for your happiness to arrive from the outside is like waiting for the sun to rise in the west. You'll be standing there a long time. And you'll miss the real sunrise that's already happening within you.

You don't need anyone else to change in order for you to be happy, despite what you keep telling yourself.
What needs to shift is how you see yourself and situations.

That shift begins with one powerful choice: Looking within first, often, and always.

Waiting for your happiness to come from other people or external factors is a trap. And you'll keep falling into it until you realize the common denominator in every situation... is you.

That doesn't mean it's all your fault. Or, anyone's fault. It only means you hold the power to change your experiences if you're willing to look inward.

The Unwillingness to Shift Our Perspective

One of the biggest barriers to growth is our own stubbornness. Let's be real, most of us are so convinced that the problem lies with someone else that we never even pause or question how we're showing up.

We point fingers, replay stories, and go down the list of how someone else messed up... but rarely do we ask:

- "How did I contribute to this situation?"
- "What role am I playing in the dynamic?"
- "Is my reaction making this better or worse?"
- "What truth am I avoiding about myself?"
- "How are my emotions and need-to-be-right affecting my perspective?"

We get so busy talking about what "they" did wrong that we don't take time to recognize the parts of ourselves that might be hurting the relationship.

That unwillingness to reflect is often what keeps us stuck. You cannot change what you refuse to own.

Time for Honest Self-Evaluation

Here's a challenge: Instead of waiting for someone else to change, try asking yourself:

- What am I holding on to that's no longer serving me or this particular relationship?
- Am I willing to see myself and the person differently?
- Do I default to blaming others because it's easier than holding myself accountable?
- What can I start doing differently concerning this person, a particular situation, and my initial response or reaction?

We know it's probably going to be a little uncomfortable at first. Growth always is.

For example, are you walking around with the same shoes on that you wore when you were eight? No, because the growth of your feet would make them uncomfortable. So, get over the discomfort and be honest with yourself. Because this is the kind of honesty that will transform your life and relationships.

Sometimes it's not what you're doing. It's what you're tolerating. Or what you're repeating. Or what you're denying in yourself.

When you dare to shift and see yourself clearly and choose to grow, that's when everything around you begins to change. Don't worry, it's a good change. One we've all been anxiously waiting for to show up.

Your Soul Is the Source

You don't need to chase peace, power, or love. You just need to tap back into it. As previously stated, it's already in you.

There is a divine power within you. The same energy that great teachers and spiritual leaders have always spoken of. You were born with it. You were created from it. And it's your divine birthright.

That inner power, God-mind, Higher Self, Universal Intelligence, is not "out there" somewhere. It's right where you are, waiting to be remembered and awakened.

When you reconnect with this Presence, everything begins to realign.
You stop hustling for love. You start embodying it.
You stop performing for acceptance. You start honoring your worth.

You already have the same power that shaped so-called miracles across generations. It's been with you the whole time. Dust your shoulders off and go get back your power.

Jason's Story: There are no coincidences in God

I didn't realize it at the time, but that night marked the beginning of everything.

I had agreed to go to church with Tina on a "date". At the time, it didn't feel spiritual. It felt casual. Maybe even random. I wasn't seeking transformation. I wasn't trying to shift my mindset. I just thought I was saying yes to getting together and having a good time.

But here's the thing about timing: when your soul is ready, life doesn't wait. It strikes at the right moment, disguised as something ordinary. That "date" wasn't about romance. It was about alignment. And it wasn't for Tina, it was for me.

I had no idea that by simply showing up, I was taking the first step toward a completely different life. It wasn't dramatic. It wasn't loud. It was a quiet, pivotal choice to honor something stirring within me, something I couldn't name yet, but could feel. That night marked a shift I wouldn't fully understand until years later.

Looking back, I now see it clearly: that moment was never about going out with Tina. It was about coming home to myself.

Because here's what I've learned, when your intuition whispers, you listen. When that quiet inner nudge tells you to move, you move. No overthinking. No second-guessing. Just trust. And that trust becomes the foundation of everything that follows.

That one step led to years of growth. Of unlearning and relearning. Of shifting from seeking outside validation to standing firm in the truth that everything I needed was already within me.

Now, decades later, I'm still walking the path that moment opened up. But the difference is, I'm no longer looking for direction outside of myself. I've come to rely on the inner voice, the divine nudge, that keeps me grounded and clear. The better I listen, the better I live.

Every day, I commit to becoming a better version of myself - not for perfection, but for peace. I speak with more intention. I respond with more love. I lead with more clarity. And because of that, everything around me transforms, from my relationships, my business, my family, and my purpose.

That night at church taught me something I'll never forget: when you move on intuition, your life moves with you. And when you honor that whisper inside, you stop chasing what's outside.

So if you're waiting for a sign, this might be it.

Don't question the feeling. Don't argue with the nudge. Just take the leap of faith.

Because transformation often shows up disguised as something small or even insignificant.

But that *"small"* moment?
Might be the beginning of something *"BIG"*.

Tina's Story: Finding That Inner Voice

As a freshman in high school, I was placed in all honors classes. Expectations were high, from my teachers, my family, and myself.

I had always been a strong student, but somewhere between the distractions of boys, extracurricular activities, and figuring out who I was as a teenager, my focus started to slip.

Before I knew it, I was failing two major classes.

It didn't make sense. I understood the material. I wasn't lost in class. And yet, my grades told a different story. I remember the day my teacher called my name after class. I glanced around, certain she must have been talking to someone else. But no - it was me.

She handed me a warning slip: if I didn't show up differently or shift, I was surely going to fail her class.

I stood there stunned. Embarrassed. A wave of panic hit me.
How did I get here?
What am I going to tell my mom?
What will happen if I fail?

On my walk to the bus stop, I replayed the conversation over and over in my head. But instead of going home and immediately figuring it out, my first instinct was to ask my friends. Surely they would know what I should do. I wanted them to tell me it wasn't as bad as it sounded, to give me a shortcut, or to assure me I'd be fine without having to make big changes. I sought advice, encouragement, even a rescue plan. But no matter who I asked, their words didn't bring me the relief I was hoping for.

That night, for the first time, I gave myself space to be alone with my thoughts. Looking back, I guess you could call it prayer, but to me, it was self-reflection. I began to have a real conversation with myself - questioning who I was, what I was doing, and how I had let things get this far.

And then something shifted.

I started to see, with absolute clarity, the things I needed to start doing, as well as the things I needed to stop. I got out of bed, grabbed a notebook, and wrote down a plan. In that moment, I awakened something inside me. It was as if the inner Tina had been waiting for me to show up all along.

Before going to bed, I went to the bathroom, and I caught a glimpse of myself in the mirror. My eyes locked on my reflection, and it felt like time froze. In that stillness, I realized the truth: everything I needed was already within me. The courage. The discipline. The strength. The focus. It had always been there, I just hadn't been listening. I had been looking for that from others.

That night, I made a vow to myself. Together, the Tina I saw in the mirror and the Tina I felt inside erased the weight of the past and began shaping the future. I no longer needed anyone else to tell me who I was or what I could do. I had found my own voice - and I trusted it.

Sometimes, life shakes you awake in the most unexpected ways. That warning from my teacher wasn't a punishment. It was an invitation, an invitation to stop seeking validation from others and start trusting the one person who knows me best: me.

And once I understood that, no one would ever decide my future for me, but me!

While our experiences were different, the lesson was the same. Both of us had moments when we realized that the answers we were searching for weren't "out there" somewhere, but were already inside of us. Jason's moment came when he stopped viewing a single decision as random chance and recognized it as divine timing. Mine came when I stopped asking everyone else for advice and started trusting my own inner voice. In our own ways, we each discovered that self-trust and inner alignment aren't just nice ideas - they're the foundation for every relationship we have, including the one with ourselves. And once we learned that truth, everything in our lives began to shift.

Awareness That Your Self-Relationship Might Need Some Attention

Here are a few signs that your relationship with yourself could use a mindset shift and a little more honest reflection:

- You constantly judge yourself.
- You downplay your achievements.
- You seek approval before making decisions.
- You feel uncomfortable being alone with your thoughts.

- You don't know what brings you joy outside of others.
- You second-guess yourself when making decisions about unhealthy relationships.
- You are confused about the unsavory situations and circumstances in your life.
- You blame others for the type of relationship you have with them.

Healing starts with becoming aware. You can't change what you're not willing to acknowledge.

Strengthen Your Self-Relationship

Here are three simple practices you can begin today to reconnect with the most important relationship you'll ever have:

1. The Mirror Talk

Every morning, look into your own eyes and say aloud:

"I see you. I love you. I've got you. Yesterday doesn't matter, right here, right now does."

This is not just feel-good fluff. You're reprogramming your subconscious and reminding yourself that you're not alone, you're not half, and you're not insignificant. You're everything you need, perfect, whole, and complete.

2. Silent Check-ins

Set a timer once or twice a day to pause and ask:

"How am I really feeling right now?"
"What do I need in this moment?"

"What do I need to see differently to make me feel at peace and in control?"

"Will focusing on something negative make me feel better or worse?"

Most of us never stop to ask. But your soul is always speaking and receiving, if you give it space to be heard and felt.

3. Evening Journaling Prompt

Write a response to this question:

"What am I expecting others to give me that I haven't given myself? And Why?"

This prompt can bring clarity and release. Many breakthroughs start with this one question.

Affirmation from the God-Mind Within

My Divine Self is constructing new thought patterns of a positive nature in my mind, this moment, and I accept that they are already mine. And so it is!

You are not broken. You are shifting. Keep going. Keep growing.

Final Thought

You are not here to fix yourself; you're here to remember who you already are and be just that.
You are whole. You are powerful. And the relationship you have with yourself sets the tone for everything and everyone else in your life.

When you love yourself, not in a cliché way, but in a deep, committed, soul-connected way, you stop begging others to give what you were always meant to give yourself, love and acceptance.

The moment you return to your own center, everything else begins to shift.

And it all begins with one brave decision:

To stop looking for love in all the wrong places. Meaning, searching outside of yourself instead of looking within. How can others love you when you really don't know or love yourself? Just saying?

My key takeaways or thoughts:

_____

_____

_____

_____

_____

_____

_____

_____

_____

_____

_____

_____

_____

_____

My strengths and personal affirmations:

_____

_____

_____

_____

_____

_____

_____

_____

_____

_____

_____

_____

_____

_____

_____

_____

_____

My promise to myself:

_____

_____

_____

_____

_____

_____

_____

_____

_____

_____

_____

_____

_____

_____

Things I currently struggle with that need more focus
(To release or change):

_____

_____

_____

_____

_____

_____

_____

_____

_____

_____

_____

_____

_____

_____

My Goals, Ideas, and Commitment:

_____

_____

_____

_____

_____

_____

_____

_____

_____

_____

_____

_____

_____

_____

_____

TWO

THE PEOPLE WHO SHAPED YOU AND THE PATTERNS YOU NEVER NOTICED

Your first lessons in love, trust, and disappointment didn't come from a textbook. They came from the people who raised you, laughed with you, and sometimes hurt you. Those early experiences are still steering you today, even when you think you're in control.

After the relationship with yourself, the next most impactful relationships in your life are those with family and friends. These are the people who know you best. The ones who have seen your highs and lows, and in many cases, helped shape your beliefs, habits, and emotional responses. That's also what makes these relationships the most complicated at times.

Family and friends often reflect back to us our old patterns, our wounds, and our past. These are not just the people in your life. They are the people who helped build the blueprint of how you relate to others.

The question is not whether your family or friends are perfect. None of us are. The real question is this: How do you show up in those relationships now?

Stop Holding Others Responsible for Your Peace

It is easy to fall into the trap of blaming our family for how we turned out.
We hear things like:

- If my parents had been more supportive, I would be different.
- If my siblings respected me more, we would get along better.
- If my friends didn't drain me, I would not feel so resentful.

- If my family took the time to know the real me, I wouldn't have to react the way I do.

And while those thoughts might feel justified, the truth is this:

You cannot move forward while holding someone else responsible for your emotional well-being.

Even if your parents or family were toxic. Even if your friends betrayed your trust. Even if your boundaries were never seemingly respected. You still have the power to choose how you engage now. You get to rewrite the script. It is your view and your perspective. You get to choose how you see it and how it will impact your here-and-now. Who holds the power over your life, you or the other person?

That does not mean pretending everything is okay when it is not. It means learning how to set boundaries, manage your energy, and create space for the relationships you want to grow and the ones you may need to release. It means meeting people where they are and loving them regardless of how you want them to be.

Your Energy Is the Conversation

One of the core truths in life is that your energy speaks before you do. Your thoughts, feelings, and expectations are already communicating to others long before you open your mouth.

When you think about someone, speak about someone, or react to someone, your energy is either attracting harmony or tension.

This is why changing how you see a person can begin to shift the dynamic between you and them.

If you want more respect, begin to see your relationship with them as capable of expressing respect.
If you want peace, see them as someone who can meet you in a space of understanding.
If you want distance, bless them and release them in love.

Everything you desire must first be created within.

Honoring the Past Without Being Stuck in It

Some family patterns run deep. They were passed down like furniture, carried from generation to generation without question. But just because something has been your "normal" does not mean it is right or healthy. Or vice versa, just because it has always been a part of your family, doesn't mean you have to fight against it. You can choose to find a happy medium. Respect can go a long way.

You may have been taught not to express emotion, learned that conflict or disagreements are dangerous, or even grown up believing love must be earned.

All of that can change. But not by blaming. Only by acknowledging and choosing something new, different, and positive.

Give yourself permission to say:

- That may have been how I was raised, but it is not who I choose to be.
- That may have been how we used to talk, but it is not how I choose to communicate now.
- That may have been the dynamic, but it is no longer what I will accept.
- Certain family behavior may have been passed down, but I can tweak it to make it healthier and better to fit who I am now.

Changing your relationship with family and friends is not about changing them.

It is about standing in the truth of who you are now and choosing how you will respond, love, and connect without bitter feelings or negative ways of viewing them or the past. Shifting requires you to see things from a higher level of awareness to create healthier relationships.

How to Evaluate the Health of Your Connections

Here are a few questions to help you assess whether your relationships with family and friends are supportive or draining:

- Do I feel emotionally safe being myself around them?
- Do I leave conversations feeling uplifted or depleted?
- Am I constantly walking on eggshells to avoid conflict?
- Do I feel free to say no without guilt?
- Is this relationship based on love or obligation?
- Am I seeing things through the lens of past hurt or positive beginnings?
- Am I open to new ways in old relationships?

This is not about judging others. It is about being honest with yourself. Yet, realizing that your past mindset may have altered the way you viewed things. Therefore, growth and understanding must be a driving force in the more grown-up version of you. Holding people for what you view as past injustices keeps you tied to them and the experience. Recognize that they did the best they could with their own level of understanding and awareness of who they were. Release them and let them go. This opens the door for better situations and relationships to grow. Holding grudges holds you down.

When you value your peace, your time, and your energy, you stop being stuck in blame or the past and create a new future.

Boundaries

Not every relationship is meant to stay close. And that is okay. Some people are part of your life for a season. Others for a lifetime.

Your job is not to cling to every connection out of guilt. Your job is to protect your mental and spiritual space so you can grow.

If someone consistently crosses your boundaries, drains your joy, or manipulates your kindness, it is okay to:

- Take space
- Reduce contact
- Speak your truth with respect and clarity
- End the relationship if necessary

You are not a bad person for outgrowing someone. Just make sure you're growing, not holding grudges or passing judgment.

You are striving to become a self-aware person who is making a conscious choice for a positive mindset and growth.

Better Family Relationships

Here are three things you can do to bring more balance and clarity to your family and friend connections.

1. The Energy Scan

Take a few minutes after any phone call or visit to ask:

How do I feel right now?
Did I shift my mindset about this person and allow healing and a healthier connection to take place?

Did I shrink or expand in their presence?

Was my peace and well-being maintained?

This will help you identify who energizes you and who drains you.

2. Setting Healthy Boundaries

Use this when setting a boundary. Keep it honest, clear, and simple:

Is this what I want?
Am I negotiating my non-negotiables?
Does this make me feel uncomfortable? And if so, why? Is it because of past experiences, ego, or judgment of others?

Am I doing what I don't like to be done to me?

Is this boundary honoring me or looking to hurt someone else?

It is about honoring everyone's needs respectfully.

3. Visualization

Picture the person you have tension with. In your mind, surround them with a white light. Say silently:

I release you with love. I release this tension. I choose peace.

This simple shift in energy can bring surprising results.

Jason's Story: Your Start Doesn't Determine Your Finish

Growing up as the youngest of three sisters, I was surrounded by love. My sisters were my protectors, always making sure I felt safe, seen, and supported. And it wasn't just them. My parents poured into me with that same level of care. I was fortunate enough to grow up in a home where love, respect, and emotional safety were the norm, not the exception.

My environment shaped how I viewed the world, my relationships, and friendships later in life. When I went out to make friends, I naturally gravitated toward people who mirrored the energy I had been raised with. I looked for kindness, mutual support, and authenticity. Not because I had a checklist, but because my spirit recognized what "safe" felt like.

And when a friendship or relationship started off with those qualities but eventually shifted into something less supportive or misaligned, I didn't hesitate to let it go. Not out of pride or anger, but because I already knew what it felt like to be loved the right way. I didn't feel the need to chase after acceptance or stay where I wasn't genuinely valued.

But don't misunderstand me. Having a strong foundation didn't mean I had all the answers.

There were still lessons I had to learn on my own. I had to make my own mistakes, fall into friendships that didn't serve me, and figure out who I was outside of my family. Growth is personal, and no foundation, no matter how strong, can teach you everything. Still, I'm grateful for the emotional grounding I started with.

Now, maybe your story is different. Maybe you didn't grow up with that kind of support. Maybe your foundation felt shaky or even non-existent. But I want you to hear this clearly: you are not doomed. You still have the power to build yourself up from wherever you started.

You get to choose who you become.

As you grow and evolve, one of the hardest things to face is how others perceive you, especially those who've known you the longest. Family often holds onto outdated versions of you. They remember who you used to be, not who you're becoming. And sometimes, they'll try to pull you back not out of malice, but because your growth makes them uncomfortable with their own stagnation.

It's your job to reintroduce yourself not with anger, but with confidence.

When friendships begin to fall away or relationships feel strained, know that it's not always a sign of failure. Sometimes, it's confirmation that you're moving into a new chapter. You're not obligated to stay close to people just because you've known them a long time. Growth requires alignment, and not everyone can (or will) grow with you.

And that's okay.

Tina's Story: Your Past Can Help or Harm You

I remember having a childhood friend who was shy, soft-spoken, kind, and reserved. We lost touch for several years, but as adults, we ran into each other again. The moment she began to speak, I barely recognized the person I used to know.

She was now outspoken, loud, aggressive, and, to be honest, a little rude. As we talked, I could feel her energy was guarded and heavy. Her view of the world, people, and relationships was drenched in negativity.

Over time, through several encounters, I learned why. She had been through relationships where she felt abused, taken advantage of, and silenced. Her childhood, unbeknownst to me, was filled with hurt and pain from her parents. Her self-worth had been stolen from her, and she was out for revenge. So she decided she would never allow that to happen again. Every relationship she had from that point on would be on her terms. She equated compromise with weakness. She spoke her mind without filter, believing it was "speaking her truth," even if it cut deep.

But here's what I saw:
Her pain had become her identity, and her defense had turned into a self-imposed prison.

She couldn't see how holding on to hurt, anger, and mistrust had poisoned her from the inside out.

However, it was eye-opening for me. In that moment, I realized something powerful: We can view our experiences as lessons to strengthen us or as weapons to destroy us. And whatever we hold onto, good or bad, the world eventually becomes for us.

I thought about my own life. There were people I disliked. People who had hurt me. People I wanted to "get back" at. Family members and friends, I felt, had betrayed me. I thought holding on to those memories and resentments was important because I wasn't letting them off the hook.

But I saw clearly that it did the opposite. Holding on tied me to them and to the pain.

So I made a choice. I chose to forgive. I chose to release. I chose to move forward without the extra baggage. And once I did, everything changed. My view of those people shifted. The hurt lost its grip on me. My soul was free to move in love instead of hate.

I live by that truth to this day: *What you think of me and how you feel about me is on you.*

Now, does that mean no one ever gets under my skin? Absolutely, not! There are still moments when someone ruffles my feathers. But now, I pause. I do the self-talk. I bless them, release them, and if necessary, limit my interaction with them. Because I know their actions are a reflection of what's going on in their soul, shaped by their experiences, and have nothing to do with me. It is not a reflection of my worth or who I am. Thank God! For growth.

My job is to protect my peace, stay in love, and keep elevating to a higher level of awareness. That takes work. It takes constant attention and intention. And I am fully committed to doing the work, because loving and choosing me means loving and choosing others, even if they don't always choose me back. That's on them.

Jason's story is about showing up the same way no matter where you are. Mine's a little different, but it still comes down to how life experiences shape us. In our own ways, we learned that the way we show up in relationships begins with the way we see ourselves. Jason's experience taught him the value of building trust and connection by showing up as his true self in every space. My journey revealed the power of releasing past hurts so they no longer control how I love or interact with others.

Affirmation for Family and Friendship Harmony

I choose to surround myself with people who see me clearly and love me fully. I honor those I must love from a distance, and I bless the space I now create for peace, growth, and true connection. And so it is!

Final Thought

Family and friends have shaped you, but they do not define you. You get to choose the kind of relationships you want moving forward.

You are not here to live by anyone else's version of who you should be. You are here to create relationships that align with your values, support your joy, and reflect your growth.

Whether you are healing old wounds, creating new connections, or letting go of what no longer fits, remember this:

You deserve peace, support, and love. And you are allowed to choose all three. Start by choosing them for yourself.

My key takeaways or thoughts:

_____

_____

_____

_____

_____

_____

_____

_____

_____

_____

_____

_____

_____

_____

My strengths and personal affirmations:

_____

_____

_____

_____

_____

_____

_____

_____

_____

_____

_____

_____

_____

_____

_____

_____

_____

My promise to myself:

_____

_____

_____

_____

_____

_____

_____

_____

_____

_____

_____

_____

_____

Things I currently struggle with that need more focus
(To release or change):

_____

_____

_____

_____

_____

_____

_____

_____

_____

_____

_____

_____

_____

_____

My Goals, Ideas, and Commitment:

_____

_____

_____

_____

_____

_____

_____

_____

_____

_____

_____

_____

_____

_____

THREE

THE 3 C'S: COLLEAGUES, CONFLICT, AND COOPERATION

The office can be more than a paycheck. It can be a place where trust is built, respect is earned, and opportunities open, simply by changing the way you connect with those you work with.

Whether you work in a corporate office, run your own business, or collaborate with others in creative or service-based environments, one truth is constant. The way you relate to others professionally directly impacts your peace, your productivity, and your potential.

Many of us spend more time with colleagues and co-workers than with our families. These daily interactions influence how we feel, how we grow, and in some cases, how we see ourselves. That is why it is so important to pay attention to the energy you bring into your professional spaces, and the energy you allow in return.

Your Job Is Not Just What You Do, But How You Do It

You may have been taught that work is just about tasks and performance. But work is also about relationships. And in some cases, those relationships are where your greatest lessons, challenges, and opportunities for growth appear.

In the workplace, you may encounter:

- Miscommunication
- Personality clashes
- Power struggles
- Unspoken expectations
- Different working styles

Just to name a few. These are not signs that something is wrong with you or your career. They are signals inviting you to grow in self-awareness, emotional intelligence, and communication.

How you handle difficult co-workers, strained team dynamics, or leadership challenges says more about your mindset than your resume.

What's Showing Up?

Metaphysical teachings remind us that your outer world reflects your inner state. Your relationships at work are often mirrors showing you parts of yourself you may not see.

- The colleague who constantly interrupts may reflect where you feel or have felt unheard.
- The manager who micromanages may reflect your own need for control because of past experiences.
- The teammate who avoids accountability may reveal where you have not spoken up for your boundaries.

This does not mean you are to blame for others' behavior. It means their behavior gives you insight into how you respond, react, and relate.

Instead of asking, "Why is this happening to me?"
Ask, "What is this revealing to me and about me?"

When you take responsibility for your part in any professional dynamic, you regain your power. You no longer wait for someone else to shift or change to make things better. You begin showing up differently, responding differently, and creating better relations differently.

Respect is Earned Through Energy and Clarity

Respect is not just about job titles or seniority. It is about the way you carry yourself. It is about how you speak, how you listen, how you lead, and how you treat others.

When you walk into a room with self-respect, people feel it. When you speak with clarity and kindness, people hear it. When you communicate with intention instead of reactivity, people notice.

This is not about being perfect. It is about being aware and aligned.

Here are a few questions to reflect on:

- Am I approachable and open to collaboration and communication?
- Do I speak with confidence or hesitate out of fear?
- Do I bring solutions, or do I just highlight problems?
- Am I clear in my communication, or do I expect others to guess what I mean?

You do not have to be the loudest voice in the room to be respected. But you do have to know your worth and communicate it through your presence.

Professional Growth Requires Emotional Maturity

You may be great at what you do, but if you lack emotional maturity, your growth will be limited. Emotional maturity at work looks like:

- Knowing when to speak and when to stay silent
- Taking feedback without defensiveness
- Managing your emotions instead of letting them run the show
- Leading with curiosity instead of ego
- Being aware when you are projecting instead of dealing with stress

It is not always easy. But it is necessary if you want meaningful connections and leadership that makes an impact.

The more you grow emotionally, the easier it becomes to navigate challenges, advocate for yourself, and create a workplace culture where respect, collaboration, and creativity thrive.

Jason's Story

Early in my professional career, I started out as a field technician. I was known around the office for being dependable, professional, and easy to talk to. I always tried to keep the mood light, cracking jokes when appropriate, showing up with a good attitude, and, most importantly, getting the job done. That balance made people comfortable around me, and it showed.

What I didn't realize at the time was that I was building something more powerful than a reputation. I was building trust.

Customers started requesting me by name. They didn't just want "a tech." They wanted Jason. Not because I was the best at problem-solving, but because of how I made them feel. That was when I learned one of the most important lessons of my career.

One of my managers once told me: "Before you fix the problem, you fix the person." That hit me. Hard.

Think about it, when someone calls your company, it's rarely because they're having a good day. Their system is down. Their boss is on their back. There's pressure to fix the issue now. They're stressed. Anxious. Frustrated. When I showed up, my first job wasn't technical; it was emotional.

I had to assure them. Calm the chaos. Let them know, "Hey, I've got you. I'm here now, and we're going to figure this out."

Whether I could fix the issue on the spot or not, people felt better simply because they felt heard, respected, and understood.

That one mindset shift changed everything for me.

While other techs focused solely on the seeming problem, I focused on the people. And the people noticed. That's why they kept requesting me. That's why my name was passed around, not because I worked miracles, but because I made people feel safe and respected in moments of stress.

Back at the office, some coworkers couldn't understand why I was always getting called back to the same accounts. They thought it was luck or favoritism. But it wasn't that. It was about relationships.

Sometimes people don't even remember what I did. They just remember how I made them feel.

And here's the thing: professionalism isn't just about what you wear or how well you do your job. It's about your mindset. How you carry yourself. How you treat others, especially under pressure. I've dealt with my fair share of irrational clients, hot-headed managers, and high-stress moments. But if I could keep my cool, speak with kindness, and stay grounded in who I am, I found that people almost always responded in kind.

Respect is reciprocal. And leadership, at its core, is relational.

That's why I've always chosen to show up as the same Jason in every area of my life. I don't switch masks depending on whether I'm with my family, at work, or out in public. I believe that alignment creates peace and peace creates power.

Who you are is your most valuable asset.
Don't lose that trying to "fit" into different environments.

Because you are the only constant in every space you enter.
And when you lead with emotional intelligence and integrity, people notice. Even if they can't always explain why.

Tina's Story

One of the biggest problems in both business and life is that people sometimes judge you before they even know you. And then they treat you based on that judgment, their own limited understanding, and, let's just say it, their immaturity.

When I started my first job in business as a young, enthusiastic teenager, I was excited. I had been lucky enough to work with some wonderful people in the past, so I thought this would be no different. But on this particular day, I met my first office bully.

I was the assistant to the assistant, and we'll call her Sharon. My instructions were to check in with her each day instead of my official supervisor. From the very beginning, I could feel her negative energy. She wasn't warm. She wasn't welcoming. She was younger than the women I had worked with before and carried herself in a way that felt unprofessional.

Every morning, she started the day with a list of "don'ts" in a sharp, condescending tone. She criticized everyone, including me. I couldn't figure out why, she didn't know me, and I certainly didn't know her.

Then one day, she loudly blamed me for something I hadn't done. The embarrassment hit me instantly, and underneath it, anger started to boil. I knew how to deal with bullies my own age, but an older coworker in a position of authority? That was new territory. Soon, I started dreading work. Her words got in my head, and I noticed my mood and productivity slipping.

One morning, I was sitting at my desk typing when she walked up and began another one of her rants. But this time, something inside me spoke up:

"This is not who you are. You are a good person and a hard worker. You decide how people will treat you. You decide how people will talk to you. And you will stop this nonsense today, professionally and respectfully, but for good."

I stood up, looked her in the eye, and calmly, but unapologetically, told her I would no longer tolerate being spoken to that way. I asked her directly if I had done something to cause her behavior toward me and, if so, to please tell me. My tone was respectful, but my boundary was clear.

From that moment on, I walked into work differently. I smiled more. I talked to people again. I enjoyed my job. And soon enough, Sharon was removed from her position.

But here's the real takeaway: the situation didn't change first, I did. Truth be told, I never even wished for her to be gone. Won't He do it!

Jason's story in this chapter is about fixing the person before fixing the problem. Mine is about fixing *me* before I could deal with the problem. Once I shifted my perspective and stood in my own confidence, everything completely changed.

Healthy Workplace Relationships

Here are some things you can do to improve your relationships at work or in business collaborations.

1. The Neutral Observer Practice

Before reacting to someone's behavior, pause and ask:

What story am I telling myself about this situation?
What assumptions am I making?
How would I respond if I viewed this neutrally, without taking it personally?

This creates space for a thoughtful response rather than an emotional reaction.

2. Professional Grounding Affirmation

Use this before meetings, interviews, or team discussions:

I bring value. I am prepared. I can and will communicate my ideas effectively. I respect others, and others respect me. All my interactions and relations will be harmonious and on one accord. I remain grounded in peace, regardless of what others bring into the room. I think, feel, and talk positively about everyone and everything. We are all one and working as a team. Cooperation is our mission and is being fully expressed by everyone.

Your energy sets the tone before you even speak.

3. The One Conversation Rule

If something is bothering you at work, commit to kindly addressing it directly with the person involved before discussing it with others. Do not pass judgment or have negative expectations. See the outcome you want, where the issue(s) have been resolved and all is well. This builds trust and eliminates unnecessary drama.

You Attract What You Expect

If you constantly expect conflict, discord, disrespect, or chaos, your energy will subtly invite those patterns to continue.
If you begin expecting harmony, cooperation, and opportunity, you open channels for those experiences to manifest.

As one metaphysical principle states, thought is energy, and energy creates form.

Your mindset shapes the professional atmosphere around you.

Don't believe us? Try it. Before you go into your next meeting, say the above affirmation. Raise your vibration and energy to one of cooperation and love. Think and speak positively, then be open and aware if anything is different.

Speak life into your day. Speak peace into your space. Your job is not just a place where you work. It is a space where you grow and learn.

Affirmation for Professional Peace and Power

I am calm, clear, and confident in all my professional interactions. I attract collaborative energy, respectful communication, and opportunities that align with my growth. I trust that I am equipped for every connection and conversation. I am emotionally mature and realize opinions are subjective, not personal. And so it is!

Final Thought

Your work environment is not just about getting things done.
It is also where you practice patience, grow in self-awareness, and learn to communicate with integrity.

You may not be able to control your colleagues or the company culture, but you can always choose how you show up.

When you shift to a positive mindset: Stand in your values. Speak your truth with grace. Protect your peace without apology.

The energy you bring to the table will do more for your success than any job title ever could.

Respect begins with you. Let others follow your example.

My key takeaways or thoughts:

_____

_____

_____

_____

_____

_____

_____

_____

_____

_____

_____

_____

_____

_____

My strengths and personal affirmations:

_____

_____

_____

_____

_____

_____

_____

_____

_____

_____

_____

_____

_____

My promise to myself:

_____

_____

_____

_____

_____

_____

_____

_____

_____

_____

_____

_____

_____

_____

_____

_____

Things I currently struggle with that need more focus
(To release or change):

_____

_____

_____

_____

_____

_____

_____

_____

_____

_____

_____

_____

_____

_____

My Goals, Ideas, and Commitment:

_____

_____

_____

_____

_____

_____

_____

_____

_____

_____

_____

_____

_____

_____

_____

FOUR

MONEY, DEGREES, CARS, CLOTHES. THEY CAN BE SYMBOLS OF SUCCESS OR SILENT SOURCES OF STRESS.

Your relationship with what you have, or think you don't have, shapes more than your bank account. It shapes your peace of mind. And when you shift the relationship you have with those things, abundance has a way of finding you without stress or strain.

Let's talk about something many people do not like to admit. Your relationship with money, education, and material things is deeply emotional. It reflects your sense of worth, your beliefs about success, and the hidden stories you carry from childhood, culture, and past experiences.

This chapter is not about teaching you how to chase material wealth. It is about how to shift your mindset so that you can stop struggling with your relationship to money, learning, and physical possessions, and start aligning with peace, flow, and abundance.

Money and Material Things Are Mirrors

Most people think of money as numbers in a bank account. But in metaphysical terms, money is energy. It is a reflection of how open or closed you are to receiving. It is also a mirror that reveals how you truly feel about yourself.

If you believe that abundance is hard to earn, you will always feel like you are working too hard for too little. If you believe that wealth is for others but not for you, you will subconsciously sabotage financial opportunities. If you were taught that having material things is selfish or greedy, you may reject prosperity while secretly longing for more.

It is not just about what you want. It is about balance. It is about what you believe you deserve. It is about having those things, but not letting them define you. And those beliefs often stem from the past.

Rewriting Old Stories Around Value and Worth

Here are some common stories people carry without even realizing it:

- I have to work twice as hard just to prove myself.
- People like me do not get ahead.
- Education is the only way to be respected.
- If I have too much, others will judge me.
- I always mess things up when I start doing well.

These beliefs create invisible walls between you and the abundance you desire.

You can want financial freedom, but if you do not believe you are worthy of it, you will always block it.

No matter what your past relationship with these things may have been, realize that every story can be rewritten.

Prosperity Starts in the Mind

From the metaphysical perspective, all outer wealth begins with inner alignment. It is taught that thought is energy. When your thoughts are focused on lack, you attract more of it. But when your thoughts align with trust, gratitude, and expansion, your outer life begins to reflect that shift.

Prosperity is not just a material condition. It is a spiritual vibration. It begins with how you think, speak, and feel about yourself and what you believe is possible.

When you believe that your supply comes from Divine Source - not from the economy, your job, or another person - you step into a new relationship with wealth.

One that is free from fear and full of flow.

Education and Knowledge as Gateways to Growth

Your relationship with learning also reveals your mindset. Do you seek knowledge to impress others? Or do you see learning as a sacred path to your growth?

True intelligence is not found in memorizing facts. It is found in aligning with your inner knowing, using spiritual intuition, and trusting the Divine Mind within you to guide your decisions.

Never stop learning. But also remember that your highest teacher is already inside you.

Jason's Story

Understanding how you relate to these things is critical. Why? Because most of what we believe about money and success isn't something we decided for ourselves. It's learned behavior. Passed down. Picked up. Absorbed. Modeled. Very little of it is conscious thought. And yet, it drives our actions every single day.

We spend, save, chase, and fear money based on beliefs that aren't even ours, or worse, are not even true.

When I began to shift how I thought about money, everything changed.

Think about it, money is just paper. Tear it up, and it's worthless. But walk into a store with it, and suddenly it has power. Why? Because of the meaning we assign to it. The truth is, money isn't power, it's energy. Like everything else, it flows according to intention, belief, and alignment.

And here's the thing: you don't "make" money. You're not printing it. You're not generating it out of thin air.

You attract it. You align with it. It becomes revealed to you based on your energy and mindset.

If you're walking around believing "it's hard to make money," then guess what? You'll constantly struggle to experience abundance. Not because money is inherently hard to get, but because your belief system is blocking the flow.

Money flows where energy goes.

When you pick up a book or study something new, the process isn't about downloading information. It's about activating what's already inside of you. That book doesn't make you smarter; it simply pulls out what was already within you, waiting to be accessed.

I once was told by a friend of mine who holds a doctorate that having a Ph.D. doesn't make them more intelligent. It just means that they completed something. They committed, stuck with it, and ultimately finished.

That's it. Success in any area, whether it's financial, academic, or personal, isn't about being extraordinary. It's about intention, consistency, and belief.

If I'm seeking better financial understanding, and I begin studying money not just how to make it, but how to manage, respect, and multiply it I will gain that understanding. Why? Because I've made it personal. I'm not just reading to know something, I'm aligning my energy to become someone new.

The same is true for relationships.
The same is true for success.
The same is true for anything you want to experience more of in your life.

Abundance starts inside.

It's not about chasing more, it's about seeing differently.
You don't have to "get" abundance. You have to recognize it, understand it, and align with it.

The more you elevate your understanding, the more access you have.
The more aligned your energy becomes, the more life will respond to you effortlessly.

Tina Marie's Story

I had a friend who grew up in some of the toughest circumstances you can imagine. As a child, her family experienced homelessness, not once, but multiple times. She told me stories about sleeping in shelters and how the sound of people arguing in the next room was a normal part of her childhood.

When she finally got out on her own, she swore she would never live like that again. And I believed her because she was driven, smart, and hardworking. Her and her husband had well-paying careers, and from the outside, they were doing quite well for themselves.

But underneath it all, that little girl who had been afraid of losing everything was still running the show. No matter how much money they made, it was never enough for her. She refused to take vacations because she was worried and concerned about what they would do if something unexpectedly happened. She'd panic if her husband even mentioned the idea of switching jobs or starting a business. She insisted they work as many hours as possible and keep saving "just in case."

Her drive wasn't by ambition. She was driven by fear.

Her marriage became more of a business arrangement than a partnership. Eventually, the tension broke them apart.

It wasn't until after her divorce and plenty of personal development that she realized what she thought was protection was really relationship suffocation.

Our relationship with money is about what's going on inside of us. For her, it wasn't about wanting more; it was about making sure she never felt the pain of "not enough" again. But in trying to protect herself from that fear, she lost something far more valuable than money.

Jason talks about seeing money as energy, not something to chase or fear. My friend's story is a reminder that when our relationship with money comes from fear, it doesn't matter how much we have; it will never be enough.

Material Things Are Tools, Not Identities

It is okay to enjoy nice things. You are not more spiritual because you reject them. And you are not more valuable because you own them. What matters is your relationship to them. Your mindset towards their importance.

Do you use things to elevate your joy or to cover up emptiness? Do you feel guilty for wanting more, or do you see it as your birthright to expand?

It is not about what you have. It is about whether you are attached to it.

71

If you lost it all tomorrow, would you still know who you are? If the answer is yes, then you are free and not chained to the conditional relationship of money and material things.

Shift Your Relationship with Money and Material Energy

Here are three examples to help realign your relationship with money, education, and things.

1. Abundance Check-In

Ask yourself:

What is my first emotional response to the word "money"?
Do I feel joy, anxiety, guilt, excitement, or shame? Why?

Once you know your dominant emotional pattern, you can begin shifting it.

2. Daily Prosperity Affirmation

Speak this every morning:

I am open and aligned with Divine Supply. Money flows to me with ease and purpose. I release fear and make room for abundance. I am already enough. All forms of abundance are my birthright as an heir to the kingdom.

This sets a new energetic tone for the day. Welcome money, success, education, and abundance, don't worship it.

3. Declutter With Intention

Choose one area of your home and remove items that no longer serve you. Speak over each item as you let it go:

I release what no longer reflects who I am. I make room for what aligns with my purpose.

This physical act of letting go opens spiritual space for expansion.

Affirmation for Abundance and Alignment

I am a divine channel for prosperity. I trust that the Universe always supports me. What I need flows to me. What no longer serves me gently falls away. I walk in gratitude, knowing I am supplied with everything for my highest good.

Final Thought

You were never meant to struggle with lack, chase worth through achievement, or tie your value to what you own.

You are worthy because you exist.
You are abundant by nature.

You are powerful beyond what your bank account or degree can measure.

You do not need to prove anything. You only need to remember who you are.

Release the fear. Replace it with trust. And realign with the divine flow that has always been yours.

My key takeaways or thoughts:

_____

_____

_____

_____

_____

_____

_____

_____

_____

_____

_____

_____

_____

_____

_____

My strengths and personal affirmations:

_____

_____

_____

_____

_____

_____

_____

_____

_____

_____

_____

_____

_____

_____

My promise to myself:

_____

_____

_____

_____

_____

_____

_____

_____

_____

_____

_____

_____

_____

_____

Things I currently struggle with that need more focus
(To release or change):

_____

_____

_____

_____

_____

_____

_____

_____

_____

_____

_____

_____

_____

My Goals, Ideas, and Commitment:

_____

_____

_____

_____

_____

_____

_____

_____

_____

_____

_____

_____

_____

_____

_____

_____

_____

FIVE

FINDING INTIMACY WHEN YOU SEE THINGS DIFFERENTLY

In love, winning the argument can mean losing the connection. Most couples don't break up because of a lack of love, but because they can't agree on the right way to see things. What if the goal wasn't to agree, but to shift our perspective so we could gain a deeper understanding?

Let's talk about one of the most fulfilling, challenging, revealing, and misunderstood relationships of all, those romantic and intimate partnerships.

Whether you are dating, married, or somewhere in between, your intimate relationship will reveal the parts of you that still need healing, attention, or understanding. These connections have the power to bring out your greatest joy, but also your deepest insecurities. That is why learning how to develop them with awareness is essential.

You Attract What You Believe You Deserve

Before we get into communication, conflict, or connection, let's start with this.

You do not attract what you say you want.
You attract what you believe you deserve and what you are vibrating.

If you believe love must be earned, you will attract partners who make you prove your worth. If you believe you are not lovable as you are, you will attract people who mirror that. If you believe true love is painful or chaotic, you will confuse peace with boredom and chase emotional highs instead. If you believe your ex is out to get you, that will be your interactions with them. If you believe that your partner doesn't care, you will get evidence of that.

Whatever it is that you feel to be true, the universe listens and gives you signs and situations to support your belief.

Your relationship patterns are not random. They are rooted in your mindset, past experiences, and emotional conditioning. Whereas, too often, we can't move beyond them because we can't see past them.

You already know the outcome of your current situation. Let's put the ball back in your court. How will you rewrite the story or narrative?

If you want something different, you have the power to create something different. But only if you are willing to be honest with yourself about what you are still carrying and vibrating. This requires you to be open and aware. No one has the power but you. Unless you choose to give that power away and let others determine how you think, feel, act, and experience life.

It is never the situation or person that needs to change; it is always your mindset pertaining to them. You can see them, the situation, and the circumstances as opportunities to develop emotional maturity and growth in consciousness. Nothing can bother you unless you allow it.

Stop Trying to Change Them and Start Understanding You

Most relationship breakdowns happen not because two people are wrong for each other, but because both people are waiting for the other to change first.

We hear things like:

- If they would just listen better, I would feel more connected.
- If they were more affectionate, I would feel more secure.
- If they stopped shutting down, I would stop overreacting.

And while your desires are valid, there is a deeper question you must ask.

What am I bringing into this relationship that may be adding to the disconnection?

This is not about blaming yourself. It is about being responsible for your energy, communication style, reactions, and intentions.

It is easy to point out what your partner needs to fix. It is much harder to examine how your tone, your walls, your silence, or your expectations might also be part of the problem.

Real growth starts when you stop asking, "Why won't they change?" and start asking, "What can I shift in how I respond, react, or relate?" "What insecurities, past traumas, or experiences do I have that I need to work through to help me move beyond the need to change someone else?" "I want others to accept who I am. Therefore, I must respect who they are as well." "Am I too emotionally attached to the outcome that is preventing me from seeing the issue from a more positive angle?"

The Power of Perspective

Let's talk about perspective in intimate relationships.
One couple we worked with came to us on the edge of separation. They loved each other but were stuck in the same arguments, feeling misunderstood and emotionally drained.

He was a problem-solver.
She was emotionally expressive.
When she opened up, he would immediately offer solutions.
She did not want solutions; she wanted connection.
He felt unappreciated for trying to help.
She felt unseen and unheard.

The turning point came when they realized that neither of them was wrong.
They just saw things differently.

The goal was not to convince the other person to see it their way.
The goal was to understand each other's perspectives and make space for both to exist.

When they stopped trying to fix each other and started listening to learn, not listening to correct, everything began to shift.

They learned how to respect each other's views, even if they did not fully agree.
And that respect rebuilt the trust and safety they had lost.

Jason's Story

Some people date with intention. Others date out of habit, boredom, or fear of being alone. And believe it or not, the same applies to marriage. You can be married with purpose or without it. You can be legally committed and emotionally disconnected. You can say you want love, peace, and partnership, but still create chaos without even realizing it.

Here's why:
You don't attract what you want you attract what you are.

People say all the time, "I want someone who's loyal, calm, emotionally available, successful, spiritual, grounded..."
But your energy, your mindset, your frequency might be radiating something entirely different.

You could be unconsciously saying, "Give me chaos."
Why? Because maybe you've learned to feel valuable by fixing things. Maybe your identity is tied to "saving" someone. If a relationship is too peaceful, you might subconsciously sabotage it because peace doesn't activate the version of you that feels useful.

It sounds strange, but it happens more often than people admit.

Here's what I've learned:
Healthy, joy-filled relationships take work.

And not just the work of "finding the right one."
I'm talking about the inner workings, the education, the awareness, the clarity to know what you truly want... beyond what society, family, or past trauma told you to want.

Most people have never taken the time to define love for themselves.
They don't know what their ideal relationship looks like, feels like, or requires of them. So they keep repeating the same patterns and wondering why nothing changes.

This isn't about blaming you, it's about ownership.
You are the only person who shows up in all of your relationships. So until you shift your mindset, your patterns will follow you from one person to the next.

You attract what you believe you deserve.
Not what you say you want.
Not what's on your vision board or in your prayer journal.
You attract at the level of your consciousness.

That's why clarity is everything.

When you're unclear about what you want, life responds with confusion. You'll see other couples and think, "I want what they have," but you aren't doing the work required to become the version of yourself that can create that kind of relationship.

Relationships aren't hard, but they do require work. What's hard is changing you, your habits, your beliefs, your fears, your emotional triggers. And yes, that's work. Heck, everything in life requires work. You don't keep attracting the "wrong" people by accident. The universe mirrors your internal world. And if you're not aligned with the love you want, you'll keep pulling in people who reflect your inner misalignment.

Even if the perfect partner showed up today to bring love, security, and emotional intelligence, you might not be able to keep them. Why?

Because you're not operating at the frequency that matches them.

So here's the truth that shifted everything for me:

You have to become everything you desire.
Do you want consistency? Be consistent.
You want trust? Be trustworthy.
Do you want peace? Live in peace not in chaos.

The change starts with you.
And when you change, your relationships will change too.

Tina Marie's Story

When I was younger and just starting to date, I already had a clear picture in my mind of the kind of man I wanted to marry one day. I knew within me the values he had to possess. Things like kindness, integrity, respect for family, a good work ethic, confidence, unconditional love, support, and most importantly, a love for God. I wasn't interested in someone who just looked good or said the right things. I wanted someone whose actions lined up with who they claimed to be.

Because I knew what I wanted, I also knew I had to become the type of woman who could attract and mirror a man like that who was looking for the same things. That meant paying attention to my own character. How I carried myself, the way I treated people, the standards I set for my own life.

Over the years, I dated people who didn't fit those values, and I could feel the mismatch. It wasn't that they were bad people; they just weren't aligned with the life I envisioned for myself. And every time I walked away from a relationship that didn't fit, it was a reminder that settling would never lead me to the relationship and future I wanted.

Knowing who you are is powerful. Knowing your values is even more powerful. Because when you're clear on both, you naturally attract the kind of person who's not just right for you, but made for you.

Jason talks about pivoting without apology. Mine was about realizing that sometimes the pivot isn't a huge life change. However, it could be a shift in how you show up, even in small moments, that changes everything.

Your Intimate Relationship Is a Mirror

Romantic relationships bring your unhealed wounds to the surface. They can sometimes reflect what you have not yet dealt with. That does not mean your partner is causing the pain. It means the pain already existed within you.

Your partner might trigger old feelings of rejection, abandonment, or not being enough.
That is not because they are the enemy. That is because your soul is asking you to finally heal or let go of what has been buried.

It does no good to avoid emotional triggers. The goal should be to eliminate emotional triggers and regain control over yourself and your emotions. You can choose to grow through them instead of fighting against them.

Love Is a State of Being, Not Just a Feeling

According to metaphysical law, true love is not dependent on what someone else gives you. It is a reflection of the love you are already in alignment with internally.

When you come into a relationship already filled with love, peace, and joy, you are not seeking someone to complete you. You are sharing the overflow.

When you believe you are enough, you stop begging others to prove it. When you feel whole, you stop trying to fix or fill others. You become, you are in a state of being, not a state of unpredictable, irrational emotions.

Romantic Relationships

Here are three exercises you could try to strengthen your connection and protect your peace in love.

1. The Conscious Awareness Practice

Before responding in a heated moment, ask yourself: "Am I reacting to my partner or to something old this moment is reminding me of?" "Am I reacting to the day's stresses or triggers, or am I stopping to be fully present in this moment to understand and create connection?"

This helps you respond with clarity instead of emotional history. Disconnect the emotional triggers and become consciously aware.

2. The Relationship Temperature Check

Once a week, ask each other:

What is one thing I did this week that made you feel loved?
What is one thing we can do better next week?

This keeps communication open and intentional. (Stay positive, that's the focus!)

3. Perspective Journal

Take turns writing from each other's point of view about a recurring challenge. Then read it aloud together and ask:

"Did I capture how you feel?"
"What part feels misunderstood?"

This builds empathy and emotional connection. Providing clarity where it may have been missing.

Affirmation for Intimate Love

I am worthy of love that honors, understands, and grows with me. My partner is worthy of love that honors, understands, and grows within them. I give and receive love freely. I speak truthfully, listen deeply, and allow space for both our truths to exist. I create a relationship rooted in mutual respect and joy. And so it is!

Final Thought

You were not created to spend your life fixing someone or being someone's project.
You were created to love and be loved, with clarity, compassion, and conscious awareness.

No relationship is perfect. But when both people are willing to look within instead of pointing fingers, love becomes a space for healing, understanding, and joy.

You do not need to be a perfect partner, nor have a perfect partner. You need a partner who is willing to grow with you, for themselves, and alongside the relationship you are building together.

Love listens. Love learns. Love lets go of control and leans into understanding.

Let your relationship reflect what's naturally inside you.

My key takeaways or thoughts:

_____

_____

_____

_____

_____

_____

_____

_____

_____

_____

_____

_____

_____

_____

_____

My strengths and personal affirmations:

_____

_____

_____

_____

_____

_____

_____

_____

_____

_____

_____

_____

_____

_____

My promise to myself:

_____

_____

_____

_____

_____

_____

_____

_____

_____

_____

_____

_____

_____

_____

Things I currently struggle with that need more focus
(To release or change):

_____

_____

_____

_____

_____

_____

_____

_____

_____

_____

_____

_____

_____

My Goals, Ideas, and Commitment:

_____

_____

_____

_____

_____

_____

_____

_____

_____

_____

_____

_____

_____

_____

_____

SIX

REWRITING THE STORY YOU'VE BEEN LIVING

The person you want to be isn't "out there" in the future. They're already inside you, waiting for you to stop holding on to who you've been.

You are at the core of every one of your relationships. Remember that the quality of your relationships will never rise above the quality of the relationship you have with yourself.

The way you see yourself shapes how the world sees you, treats you, and connects with you. And believe it or not, it shows.

You are not just a participant in life. You are the creator of it through your thinking. And your creation begins with your identity - not who you've been, but who you are willing to become.

What Do You Want – And Who Are You?

If you want better communication, be someone who listens more and reacts less.
If you want deeper connection, be someone who is open and vulnerable.
If you want more peace, be someone who chooses to stop creating chaos.
If you want respect, be someone who walks in their values.

You don't have to fake it.
You don't have to become someone else.
But you do have to make a decision to grow beyond who you've been.

Nothing changes outside of you until something shifts within you.

Form Follows Thought

The teachings of metaphysics make it very clear: your thoughts are creative.

Every thought you hold with conviction, every belief you repeat, every mental image you focus on becomes your reality.

This is not just positive thinking. It is energetic law.

When you choose a new thought, you begin creating a new experience.

When you stop recycling limiting beliefs, you begin attracting new results.

Your outer relationships are simply the form that your inner thoughts have taken.

Change the thought, and you begin to shift the form.

This is not magic. This is awareness that leads to alignment.

Why We Struggle to Change Ourselves

Even though we know change is necessary, many people still hold tightly to who they've been.

Why? Because change feels risky. Because even pain feels familiar. Because blaming others feels easier than looking at yourself.

It's easier to say, "They need to change."

It's harder to ask, "What do I need to release, reframe, or realign within me?"

Sometimes we are so convinced that the problem lies with someone else, we never realize how much power we're giving away by refusing to examine ourselves and our part.

We get stuck in cycles:

- Waiting for someone else to apologize first
- Expecting people to meet needs we haven't voiced
- Reacting from hurt instead of intention
- Repeating patterns while saying we want change

If your relationships keep feeling the same, the question is not "Why do they keep doing this?"
The real question is "What in me is allowing, attracting, or repeating this dynamic?"

And the beautiful truth? Once you ask that question honestly, change begins.

Jason's Story

I had to learn how to become who I wanted to be.

That didn't happen overnight. It came through life experiences, challenges, failures, growth spurts, and moments of doubt. It came through professional lessons and personal evolution. And the biggest shift happened when I finally gave myself permission to change.

Let me be honest, I used to struggle with pivoting.

I'd set a goal, make a decision, or commit to a plan, and then feel trapped in it even when it no longer served me. Why? Because I thought that changing my mind meant I was being inconsistent. Because society teaches us to "stick with it," even if it's destroying us. Because I worried what people would think if I didn't follow through.

But the truth is that it's okay to pivot. It's okay to change your mind. It's okay to grow in a new direction even if it surprises people.

At this stage of my life, I pivot freely. I give myself grace. If something no longer feels aligned, I don't force it. Because at the end of the day, it's my life. I'm not living for anyone else's expectations or timelines anymore.

Yes, I've done things because other people thought it was best for me.
Yes, I've made decisions out of spite just to prove someone wrong. But I've learned those are never sustainable reasons.

Now, I make decisions because Jason wants to. Because I want to feel good. Because I want to live in peace. Because I want to be fulfilled, not just productive.

And when I do that, when I honor my truth and stay aligned with who I really am, everything in my life elevates. I love myself better. I love my wife and children better. I'm a better husband, father, friend, co-worker, and person. I have a healthier relationship with money, work, time, and even rest. Why? Because I'm being better to myself.

Becoming the best version of yourself isn't about perfection. It's about alignment. It's about the truth. It's about creating a life that feels good on the inside, not just one that looks good on the outside.

So if you're reading this and you feel stuck or unsure, let me offer you this: Sit still and ask yourself, what is it that you truly want for yourself?

Not what your parents want. Not what your friends expect. Not what looks good on paper. What do you want?

What does happiness look like for you?

Because until you answer that, you're just driving aimlessly, moving, grinding, pushing without a destination. And when you don't know where you're going, you can end up anywhere.

When you know what you want, when you're clear on your why, when you get behind the wheel with purpose, you can finally move in the right direction.

This is your invitation to do just that.

Get clear. Give yourself permission to change. And become the version of yourself you've been waiting for, not the one you've been.

Tina Marie's Story

When I first started in management, I thought being a good leader meant always having the answer. If my team asked me something, I'd give them a solution - even if I wasn't fully confident, because I didn't want to look unsure.

But over time, I realized that pretending to know everything was actually holding us back. One day, I told my team, "I don't know, but I'll find out." And instead of losing respect, they respected me more. It was a pivot in how I saw leadership. It wasn't about always being right; it was about being real.

And that's what we need in our relationships. To be REAL – Releasing Everything and Allowing Love. Be ok with not knowing everything. Be ok with not having to be right. Be ok with allowing others to take the lead. Be ok with change. Be ok with showing up to support and encourage others. Be ok with being YOU. The true, genuine, unrepeatable you.

Becoming Starts with Belief

Becoming who you want to be doesn't require a perfect plan.

It starts with one choice: to believe in the version of yourself that already exists and stop waiting for others to change.

The one who speaks with clarity, leads with love, sets strong boundaries, and chooses joy.

That version of you is not far away. It's already there, waiting for you to stop playing small and start living in alignment.

Affirmation

I release who I thought I had to be.
I step into who I was created to be.
I allow love, wisdom, and clarity to guide my relationships.
I create peace from within.
I am already enough. And I am expanding into even more.
And so it is!

Final Thought

You are not stuck.
You are evolving.
You are not broken.
You are awakening.
You are not waiting for a better life.
You are creating it.

The quality of your life will always mirror the quality of the relationship you have with yourself and the beliefs you carry.

You have more power than you've been using.
You have more peace than you've been accessing.
You have more love to give and receive than you may realize.

So stop waiting for someone else to change.
Stop expecting outside circumstances to finally line up.
And take a closer, more personal look inside.

Because the transformation you're looking for...
begins with you.

My key takeaways or thoughts:

_____

_____

_____

_____

_____

_____

_____

_____

_____

_____

_____

_____

_____

_____

My strengths and personal affirmations:

_____

_____

_____

_____

_____

_____

_____

_____

_____

_____

_____

_____

_____

_____

My promise to myself:

_____

_____

_____

_____

_____

_____

_____

_____

_____

_____

_____

_____

_____

_____

Things I currently struggle with that need more focus
(To release or change):

_____

_____

_____

_____

_____

_____

_____

_____

_____

_____

_____

_____

_____

My Goals, Ideas, and Commitment:

_____

_____

_____

_____

_____

_____

_____

_____

_____

_____

_____

_____

_____

_____

_____

_____

NOW TAKE CONTROL

For discounted bulk purchases of this book for your company, association, or conference, please email us at team@legendaryrelationship.com

To book Jason and Tina Marie for interviews, training, speaking, and keynotes, Visit legendaryrelationship.com or contact team@legendaryrelationship.com

For more books, resources, and support, visit legendaryrelationship.com

Let's Connect

Website: legendaryrelationship.com
Email: team@legendaryrelationship.com
YouTube: youtube.com/@legendaryrelationship
Instagram: instagram.com/legendaryrelationship
TikTok: tiktok.com/@legendaryrelationship
Facebook: facebook.com/legendaryrelationship
Podcast: Loving Beyond The I Do